Museum Indian, William Lutley Sclater

List of the Batrachia in the Indian museum

Museum Indian, William Lutley Sclater

List of the Batrachia in the Indian museum

ISBN/EAN: 9783337306038

Printed in Europe, USA, Canada, Australia, Japan

Cover: Foto ©Andreas Hilbeck / pixelio.de

More available books at **www.hansebooks.com**

Museum Indian, William Lutley Sclater

List of the Batrachia in the Indian museum

ISBN/EAN: 9783337306038

Printed in Europe, USA, Canada, Australia, Japan

Cover: Foto ©Andreas Hilbeck / pixelio.de

More available books at **www.hansebooks.com**

LIST

OF THE

BATRACHIA

IN THE

INDIAN MUSEUM.

BY

W. L. SCLATER, M.A., F.Z.S.,

LATE DEPUTY SUPERINTENDENT OF THE INDIAN MUSEUM.

LONDON:

PRINTED BY ORDER OF THE TRUSTEES OF THE INDIAN MUSEUM.
Sm 1892.

Issued August 1892.
Price: One Rupee.

PRINTED BY TAYLOR AND FRANCIS,
RED LION COURT, FLEET STREET.

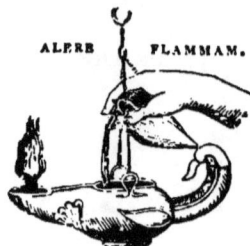

ALERE FLAMMAM.

INTRODUCTION.

The following is a List of the Batrachia contained in the Indian Museum; it is drawn up on the same plan as the List of the Snakes published in 1891.

The following Tables show the number of species and specimens preserved in the Museum :—

Number of Species.

	Indian.	Exotic.	Total.
Ecaudata	99	56	155
Caudata.................	1	21	22
Apoda	3	0	3
Total	103	77	180

Number of Specimens.

	Indian.	Exotic.	Total.
Ecaudata	1656	254	1910
Caudata.................	18	93	111
Apoda	24	0	24
Total	1698	3 47	2045

The number of species described by Mr. Boulenger in his ' Reptiles and Batrachians of British India' was 130; to these may be added :—

> 5 new species described by Mr. Boulenger and myself since the appearance of the 'Fauna of British India' —*Rana assamensis, R. limborgi, R. tenasserimensis, R. oatesi,* and *Ixalus travancoricus.*

4 species previously confounded with well-known forms now shown to be distinct—*Rana vicina, R. granulosa, Ixalus cinerascens, Bufo stomaticus.*

2 species previously unknown to the Indian fauna but since added—*Ixalus asper, Microhyla achatina.*

6 species confined to the Malay Peninsula and not recorded from British India proper—*Rana haschcana, R. plicatella, R. glandulosa, Bufo penangensis, Phrynella pollicaris, Megalophrys nasuta.*

Making in all 147 species known from British India and the Malay Peninsula; of these, as is shown in the Table above, the Indian Museum possesses specimens of 103, so that there are still 44 species unrepresented in the Museum, and of these desiderata a list is given below.

The number of type specimens in the Museum amounts to 21, of which 7 were described by Stoliczka, 5 by Anderson, 4 by Blyth, 3 by myself, and 1 each by Blanford and Jerdon; a complete list of these, together with the references to the original descriptions, will also be found below.

The arrangement and nomenclature of this list are entirely formed on Mr. Boulenger's work in the British Museum Catalogues and the Reptiles and Batrachia in the 'Fauna of British India' series, and I have to offer him further my very best thanks for a great deal of help in identifying many obscure specimens and allowing me full access to all the British Museum Collections.

The descriptions of several new species and certain novel facts in geographical distribution and synonymy will be found in a paper published in the Proc. Zool. Soc. for 1892, p. 341, which is referred to throughout the list.

The principal donors of the Batrachia in the Indian Museum are:—Dr. F. Stoliczka, Dr. J. Anderson, Dr. T. C. Jerdon, and Mr. W. T. Blanford from all parts of India; Col. Beddome and Mr. W. M. Daly from South India; Mr. Gammie from the Darjeeling District, and Mr. W. Theobald from Burma; and, finally, Capt. J. Butler and Messrs. S. E. Peal and J. H. Bourne from Assam.

SYSTEMATIC INDEX.

(The names of Indian and Malayan species are printed in small capitals and of exotic species in ordinary type.)

LIST OF INDIAN AND MALAYAN BATRACHIA UNREPRESENTED IN THE INDIAN MUSEUM COLLECTIONS.

Rana corrugata, Ptrs.
  ,, khasiana (Anders.)
  ,, sternosignata, Murr.
  ,, andersonii, Boul.
  ,, dobsonii, Boul.
  ,, strachani (Murr.)
  ,, leithii, Boul.
  ,, diplostica (Günth.)
  ,, phrynoderma, Boul.
  ,, lateralis, Boul.
  ,, margariana (Anders.)
  ,, humeralis, Boul.
  ,, oatesii, Boul. *
  ,, formosa (Günth.)

Micrixalus sarasinorum (F. Müll.)
  ,, opisthorhodus (Günth.)
Nyctibatrachus pygmaeus (Günth.)
Nannophrys ceylonensis, Günth.
  ,, guentheri, Boul.
Rhacophorus nasutus (Günth.)
  ,, reticulatus (Günth.)
  ,, dubius, Boul.
  ,, jerdonii (Günth.)
  ,, fergusonii, Boul.
Ixalus schmardanus (Kel.)
  .. hypomelas, Günth.
  ., vittatus, Boul.
  ,, femoralis, Günth.

* Ann. Mag. N. H., Febr. 1892, p. 141, pl. ix. (Burma).

Ixalus beddomii, Günth.
  „   adspersus, Günth.
  „   travancoricus, Boul. *
Phrynella pollicaris, Boul. †
Callula macrodactyla, Boul.
Glyphoglossus molossus, Günth.
Callulella guttulata (Bly.)
Nectophryne tuberculosa (Günth.)

Bufo pulcher, Boul.
  „   hololius, Günth.
  „   macrotis, Boul.
  „   beddomii, Günth.
Leptobrachium feæ, Boul.
Megalophrys nasuta, Schlegel ‡
Uraeotyphlus malabaricus (Bedd.)
Gegenophis carnosus (Bedd.)

LIST OF THE TYPE SPECIMENS IN THE INDIAN MUSEUM,

WITH REFERENCES TO THE ORIGINAL DESCRIPTIONS.

Rana vicina, Stoliczka, Pr. A. S. B. 1872, p. 130.

Rana assamensis, W. Sclater, P. Z. S. 1892, p. 343, pl. xxiv. fig. 2.

Rana bascheana, Stoliczka, J. A. S. B. xxxix, 1870, p. 147.

Rana limborgi, W. Sclater, P. Z. S. 1892, p. 344, pl. xxiv. fig. 3.

Rana plicatella, Stoliczka, J. A. S. B. xlii, 1873, p. 116, pl. xi, fig. 1.

Rana tenasserimensis, W. Sclater, P. Z. S. 1892, p. 345, pl. xxiv. fig. 4.

Rana nigrovittata, Blyth, J. A. S. B. xxiv, 1855, p. 718.

Rana granulosa, Anderson, J. A. S. B. xl, 1871, p. 23.

Rana nicobariensis, Stoliczka, J. A. S. B. xxxix, 1870, p. 150, pl. ix, fig. 2.

Rana monticola, Anderson, J. A. S. B. xl, 1871, p. 25.

Rhacophorus maculatus, Anderson, J. A. S. B. xl, 1871, p. 27 §.

Rhacophorus tuberculatus, Anderson, J. A. S. B. xl. 1871, p. 26.

Rhacophorus cruciger, Blyth, J. A. S. B. xxi, 1852, p. 355.

Ixalus cinerascens, Stoliczka, Pr. A. S. B. 1870, p. 275.

Microhyla berdmorii, Blyth, J. A. S. B. xxiv, 1855, p. 720.

Callula variegata, Stoliczka, Pr. A. S. B. 1872, p. 111.

Bufo olivaceus, Blanford, Ann. Mag. N. H. (4) xiv, 1874, p. 35.

Bufo penangensis, Stoliczka, J. A. S. B. xxxix, 1870, p. 152, pl. ix, fig. 4.

Cophophryne sikkimensis, Blyth, J. A. S. B. xxiii, 1854, p. 300.

Hyla annectens, Jerdon, Pr. A. S. B. 1870, p. 84.

Tylototriton verrucosus, Anderson, P. Z. S. 1871, p. 423.

---

* Ann. Mag. N. H. (6) viii. p. 291 (Travancore).
† P. Z. S. 1890, p. 37 (Perak).
‡ Boulenger, Cat. Batr. Sal. p. 443 (Pinang).
§ Name changed by Boulenger to bimaculatus.

LIST

BATRACHIA

IN THE

INDIAN MUSEUM.

Order I. ECAUDATA.

Family RANIDÆ.

1. OXYGLOSSUS LIMA (Gravenh.).

Boulenger, Ind. Rept. p. 436.
Distribution—Lower Bengal, Burma, South China, Indo-China,
Malay Peninsula, and Java.

2 Moulmein	F. Stoliczka	2750-1.
1 Mergui	Mergui Exped. (Anderson)	11798.
2 Lampee, Mergui (tadpoles)	Mergui Exped. (Anderson)	11788-9.

2. OXYGLOSSUS LÆVIS, Günth.

Boulenger, Ind. Rept. p. 437.
Distribution—Burma, Malay Peninsula, Sumatra, and the Philippines.

1 Pilai, Mergui	Mergui Exped. (Anderson)	11839.
1 No loc.	No hist., A. S. B.	8991.

B

3. RANA HEXADACTYLA, Lesson.

Boulenger, Ind. Rept. p. 441.
Distribution—The Indian Peninsula and Ceylon.

3 Jaipur, Vizag. dist.	Col. R. H. Beddome	9431–3.
1 Malabar	E. Gerard [P.]	12191.
1 South India	T. C. Jerdon, A. S. B.	9122.
2 South India	Col. R. H. Beddome	10545, 10547.
9 Colombo, Ceylon	J. Anderson	9218–9, 9221, 9224, 9245,
		9250, 9252, 9260, 9262.
2 Galle, Ceylon	J. Anderson	10812–3.
2 Ceylon	Dr. E. F. Kelaart, A. S. B.	9123–4.
	(TYPES OF RANA ROBUSTA, Blyth.)	

4. RANA CYANOPHLYCTIS, Schneid.

Boulenger, Ind. Rept. p. 442.
Distribution—Throughout South Asia from Arabia to the Malay Peninsula, and from the Himalayas to Ceylon.

13 Pishin, Baluchistan	Persian Coll. (Blanford)	3513–5, 9941-50.
1 Ghistigan, Baluchistan	Persian Coll. (Blanford)	3518.
2 Dizak, Baluchistan	Persian Coll. (Blanford)	3516-7.
1 Hunj, Baluchistan	Persian Coll. (Blanford)	9940.
4 Between Murree and Kashmir	Yarkand Exp., 1873-74 (Stoliczka)	9434-7.
3 N.W. Himalayas	Capt. Murray	10818-20.
1 Katmandu	Museum Coll.	9575.
1 Agra	Agra Museum	9040.
4 Nagpur, C. P.	Museum Coll.	9149-51, 9163.
5 Chanda, C. P.	Museum Coll.	9621-5.
4 E. of Chanda, C. P.	W. T. Blanford	9168-71.
1 Canara	Dr. F. Day	4284.
2 Mangalore	Dr. F. Day	9442-4.
2 South India	Col. R. H. Beddome	10546, 10558.
4 Ceylon	Dr. E. F. Kelaart, A. S. B.	9092, 9094-5, 9100.
2 Ceylon	H. Nevill	10782, 10784.
5 Colombo, Ceylon	J. Anderson	9228, 9230-2, 9238.
2 Orissa	F. Stoliczka	3540-1
2 Raneegunge	Museum Coll.	9359-60.
3 Burrabhoom	Museum Coll.	9326, 9328, 9338.
3 Zoological Gardens Tank, Calcutta	J. Anderson	11464-5, 11467.
1 Botanical Gardens, Calcutta	J. Anderson	9175.
1 Haldibari, Kuch Behar	Purchased	11031.
1 Garo hills, Assam	Capt. Williamson	3935.
1 Tezpur	Duflla Exped. (Godwin-Austen)	3964.
1 Goalpara, Assam	H. L. Haughton	9199.
3 Sibsagar, Assam	S. E. Peal	12860, 12863, 12867.
7 Samagooting, Assam	Capt. J. Butler	9263, 9270-1, 9286,
		9502, 9510.
2 Jergo Isle, Arakan	Marine Survey (Farrell)	12632-3.
1 Moulmein	Capt. Hood	10960.
2 No loc.	Netley Museum	1092, 4242.

5. RANA VICINA, Stol.

Stoliczka, Proc. As. Soc. Beng. 1872, p. 130 ; W. Sclater, P. Z. S. 1892, p. 342, pl. xxiv. fig. 1.
Distribution—The North-west Himalayas.

1 Murree, Himalayas, 6000 ft.	F. Stoliczka	9147.
	(TYPE OF R. VICINA, Stol.)	
1 Simla	Lieut. A. Newnham	13586.

6. RANA KUHLII, Dum. & Bibr.

Boulenger, Ind. Rept. p. 443.
Distribution—Burma, South China, and the Malay Archipelago.

7 Hotha, Yunan	Yunan Exp. (Anderson)	4171-2, 4264-5, 9399-9400, 9402.
23 Ponsee, Yunan	Yunan Exp., 1868 (Anderson)	4177, 9401, 9551-71.
1 2nd defile Irrawady	Yunan Exp., 1875 (Anderson)	10817.
1 Proome	Yunan Exp., 1868 (Anderson)	4176.
3 No loc.	Yunan Exp. (Anderson)	4168, 4170, 4263.
1 No. loc.	No hist., A. S. B.	9576.

7. RANA LATICEPS, Boul.

Boulenger, Ind. Rept. p. 444.
Distribution—Khasia hills, Assam, and Malay Peninsula.

1 Tura, Garo hills	Capt. Williamson	10962.
5 Cherrapunji, Khasia hills	J. H. Bourne	10431-5.
3 Khasia hills	T. C. Jerdon	9639-41.
1 Malacca	Raffles Museum (Davison)	13350.

8. RANA LIEBIGII, Günth.

Boulenger, Ind. Rept. p. 445 ; W. Sclater, P. Z. S. 1892, p. 343.
Distribution—The Himalayas, especially of Nepal and Sikkim, extending to Tenasserim.

1 Darjeeling	T. C. Jerdon	9580.
	(TYPE OF R. SIKIMENSIS, Jerdon.)	
1 Darjeeling	J. Anderson	9173.
1 Darjeeling	J. Gammie	9172.
	(CO-TYPES OF R. GAMMIEI, Anders.)	
2 Lachung, Sikkim, 9000 ft.	W. T. Blanford	9572-3.
3 Sikkim	Major Sherwill, A. S. B.	9577-9.
1 Tavoy	Mus. Coll.	13484.
4 No loc.	No hist.	9664-7.

9. RANA FEÆ, Boul.

Boulenger, Ind. Rept. p. 446 ; W. Sclater, P. Z. S. 1892, p. 343.
Distribution—The hills of Upper Burma and Yunan.

1 Hotha, Yunan	Yunan Exped., 1868 (Anderson)	4167.

10. RANA ASSAMENSIS, Scl. f.

W. Sclater, P. Z. S. 1892, p. 343, pl. xxiv. fig. 2.
Distribution—Hills of Assam.

1	Khasia bills	T. C. Jerdon	9574.
		(TYPE OF THE SPECIES, Scl. f.)	

11. RANA DORIÆ, Boul.

Boulenger, Ind. Rept. p. 447.
Distribution—Burma.

5	Pegu	W. Theobald	9626-8, 10491-2.
2	Mooleyit, Tenasserim, 4000-5000 ft.	Tenasserim Exped. (Limborg)	9341, 9354.
1	Meetan, 4000 ft.	Tenasserim Exped. (Limborg)	9541.
2	Ahsoon, Tenasserim	Tenasserim Exped. (Limborg)	4842-3.
3	Tenasserim	Tenasserim Exped. (Limborg)	4473-5.
2	Taing, Mergui	Mergui Exped. (Anderson)	11821, 11823.
1	Yeemeekee, Mergui	Mergui Exped. (Anderson)	11799.
1	Burma	W. Theobald	10829.

12. RANA HASCHEANA, Stol.

Stoliczka, J. A. S. B. xxxix. 1870, p. 147; W. Sclater, P. Z. S. 1892, p. 344.
Distribution—Penang.

3	Penang	F. Stoliczka	2695-7.
		(TYPES OF THE SPECIES, Stol.)	

13. RANA LIMBORGI, Scl. f.

W. Sclater, P. Z. S. 1892, p. 344, pl. xxiv. fig. 3.
Distribution—Tenasserim.

1	Meetan, Tenasserim	Tenasserim Exped. (Limborg)	5400.
		(TYPE OF THE SPECIES, Scl. f.)	

14. RANA MACRODON, Dum. & Bibr.

Boulenger, Ind. Rept. p. 448.
Distribution—Burma, the Malay Peninsula and Islands.

2	Pegu	Major Berdmore, A. S. B.	9076-7.
8	Pegu (tadpoles)	Major Berdmore, A. S. B.	9078-85.
		(TYPES OF R. FUSCA, Bly.)	
8	Meetan, Tenasserim, 3000-4000 ft.	Tenasserim Exped. (Limborg)	9533-40.
4	Tenasserim	W. Theobald	9206-9.
4	Taing, King's Isle, Mergui	Mergui Exped. (Anderson)	11790-3.
2	Malay Peninsula	Raffles Mus. (Davison)	13338-9.

15. RANA VERRUCOSA, Günth.

Boulenger, Ind. Rept. p. 448.
Distribution—Southern India.

1 Anamalai hills	Col. R. H. Beddome	2812.
2 Travancore	Col. R. H. Beddome	2819-20.

16. RANA PLICATELLA, Stol.

Boulenger, Cat. Batr. Sal. p. 26.
Distribution—Penang.

1 Penang	F. Stoliczka	9542.
	(TYPE OF THE SPECIES, Stol.)	

17. RANA TIGRINA, Daud.

Boulenger, Ind. Rept. p. 449 ; W. Sclater, P. Z. S. 1892, p. 344.
Distribution—Throughout the Indian Empire, China, and South-east Asia.

1 Rajanpur, Punjab	Dr. E. Sanders	9041.
2 Agra	Agra Museum	9025, 9039.
1 Sind	Karachi Museum [Ex.]	9227.
3 Khandalla, Bombay dist.	W. T. Blanford	9010-2.
3 Canara	Dr. F. Day	4281-3.
1 Mangalore	Dr. F. Day	9443.
1 nr. Badrachelam, Go-davery dist.	W. T. Blanford	9067.
2 Koppa, Mysore	W. M. Daly	13562-3.
3 Colombo, Ceylon	J. Anderson	9017, 9057, 9060.
3 Ceylon	Dr. E. F. Kelaart, A. S. B.	9071, 9074-5.
1 Chandbally, Orissa.	C. H. Dreyer	12572.
6 Calcutta	E. Blyth, A. S. B.	8999-9004.
5 Calcutta	J. Anderson	9028, 9030-1, 9042, 9046.
3 Botanical Gardens, Calcutta.	J. Anderson	9005, 9007, 9049.
2 Nattore, Rajshye dist.	T. R. Doucett	5576-7.
1 Goalpara	H. L. Haughton	9069.
3 Samagooting	Capt. J. Butler	9033-41, 9036.
2 Dilcosh, N.E. Cachar	J. Inglis	11371-2.
9 Hotha, Yunan	Yunan Exped. (Anderson)	4164-5, 9061-6.
7 Mandalay	Yunan Exped. (Anderson)	4175, 9020-3, 9447, 9517.
1 Mandalay	Capt. Slater	9008.
1 Proome	Yunan Exped. (Anderson)	9121
1 Penang (juv.)	F. Stoliczka	3529.
	(TYPE OF RANA GRACILIS, var. FULLA, Stol.)	
9 (Tadpoles)	No history	10803-11.

18. RANA LIMNOCHARIS, Wiegm.

Boulenger, Ind. Rept. p. 450.

Distribution—Throughout the Indian Empire and Ceylon, Southern Japan, China, Indo-China, the Malay Peninsula and Islands.

5 Katmandu, Nepal	Museum Coll.	9127-31.
1 Nagpur, C. P.	Museum Coll.	9200.
6 E. of Chanda, C. P.	W. T. Blanford	2700-5.
1 Nilgiri hills	No history.	9148.
2 Anamalai hills	Col. R. H. Beddome	10150-1.
3 South India	Col. R. H. Beddome	10223-5.
3 Ceylon	Dr. E. F. Kelaart, A. S. B.	2752, 2791-2.
6 Dacca	Col. Tytler, A. S. B.	2793-8.
1 Gauhati, Assam	Museum Coll.	9629.
3 Goalpara	H. L. Haughton	9140, 9357-8.
1 Narainpur	Col. H. H. Godwin-Austen	2878.
5 Sibsagar	S. E. Peal	2699, 2748, 10467, 10469, 10471.
1 Garo hills	Col. H. H. Godwin-Austen	9543.
2 Shillong	Duffla Exped. (Godwin-Austen)	3965-6.
6 Cherrapunji	J. H. Bourne	9413, 9415-7, 9419, 9421.
6 Samagooting	Capt. J. Butler	9136-8, 9201-2, 9205.
2 Cachar	Museum Coll.	9197-8.
3 Arakan	F. Stoliczka	3535-7.
28 Hotha, Yunan	Yunan Exped. (Anderson)	4170, 4173-4, 9301-25.
1 Ponsee, Yunan	Yunan Exped. (Anderson)	10966.
1 Yunan	Yunan Exped. (Anderson)	10330.
5 Sawaddy, nr. Bhamo	Yunan Exped. (Anderson)	9363, 9367-8, 9370, 9374.
3 Proome	Yunan Exped. (Anderson)	4178-9, 10965.
5 Pegu	Major Berdmore, A. S. B.	2799-803.
2 Pegu	W. Theobald	2682-3.
3 Rangoon	F. Stoliczka	3542-4.
1 Tenasserim	E. Gerrard [P.]	12509.
5 Moulmein	F. Stoliczka	3545-6, 3548, 3550, 3555.
8 Mooleyit, 4000-5000 ft.	Tenasserim Exped. (Limborg)	9343, 9345-6, 9348-9, 9350, 9352, 9356.
1 Tavoy	Mergui Exped. (Anderson)	11802.
1 Tavoy	Museum Coll.	12838.
7 Mergui	Mergui Exped. (Anderson)	11803-4, 11809-10, 11812-4.
4 Zedinon, Mergui	Mergui Exped. (Anderson)	11805-8.
5 Mithathoung, Mergui	Mergui Exped. (Anderson)	11829-30, 11832, 11834, 11836.
1 Taing, King Isle	Mergui Exped. (Anderson)	11845.
3 Andamans	F. Stoliczka	2732, 3538-9.
(TYPES OF R. GRACILIS, var. ANDAMANENSIS, Stol.)		
3 Andamans	G. E. Dobson	9381, 9386 7.
5 Andamans	S. Kurtz	9176-7, 8180-1, 9194.
1 Andamans	J. Wood-Mason	10436.
1 Nicobars	F. Stoliczka	2679.
(TYPE OF R. GRACILIS, var NICOBARENSIS, Stol.)		
2 Camorta, Nicobars	F. A. de Roepstorff	8887, 12550.
3 Penaug	F. Stoliczka	2678, 3533-4.
1 Penang	No history	9300.

19. RANA RUFESCENS (Jerd.).

Boulenger, Ind. Rept. p. 451.
Distribution—Malabar, in Southern India.

1 Malabar	E. Gerard [P.]	12492.

20. RANA BREVICEPS, Schneid.

Boulenger, Ind. Rept. p. 451.
Distribution—Throughout India from the Himalayas to Ceylon, extending eastwards as far as Assam.

1 Simla	F. Stoliczka	9617.
11 Agra	Agra Museum	9448, 9451, 9455, 9458, 9632-4, 9637, 9652, 9654, 9656.
3 Allahabad	J. Cockburn	9493-4, 9500.
1 Banda, N. W. P.	J. Cockburn	11460.
1 Jeypore hills, Vizag. dist.	Col. R. H. Beddome	9620.
2 Anamalai hills.	Col. R. H. Bendome	2838, 2841.
1 South India	E. Gerard [P.]	12515.
1 Ceylon	E. F. Kelaart, A. S. B.	2681.
2 Garo hills	Capt. Williamson	3933-4.
1 No loc.	C. B. Charles	10822.
1 No loc.	Col. R. H. Beddome	11565.

21. RANA BEDDOMII (Günth.).

Boulenger, Ind. Rept. p. 453.
Distribution—Forests of South India.

1 Anamalai hills	Col. R. H. Beddome	10949.
20 South India	Col. R. H. Beddome	10585, 10587, 10590, 10595, 10616, 10626-7, 10630-1, 10644, 10666, 10674, 10683, 10686, 10696, 10699, 10700, 10708, 10713, 10731.

22. RANA SEMIPALMATA, Boul.

Boulenger, Ind. Rept. p. 454.
Distribution—Malabar.

1 South India	Col. R. H. Beddome	10745.

23. RANA LEPTODACTYLA, Boul.

Boulenger, Ind. Rept. p. 454.
Distribution—Southern India.

2 Anamalai hills	Col. R. H. Beddome	2839-10.

1 Malabar	E. Gerard [P.]	12518.
28 South India	Col. R. H. Beddome	10598, 10611, 10621, 10623,
		10637-9, 10645-7, 10651-3,
		10656, 10667, 10670, 10675,
		10681, 10685, 10689, 10697,
		10707, 10712, 10719,
		10724-5, 10727-8.

24. RANA TENASSERIMENSIS, Scl. f.

W. Sclater, P. Z. S. 1892, p. 345, pl. xxiv. fig. 4.
Distribution—Tenasserim.

| 5 Tenasserim | Tenasserim Exped. (Limborg) | 10429-30, 10495-7. |
| | (TYPES OF THE SPECIES, Scl. f.) | |

25. RANA MACRODACTYLA (Günth.).

Boulenger, Ind. Rept. p. 455.
Distribution—Burma and South China.

| 1 Pegu | W. Theobald | 2698. |

26. RANA GRACILIS, Gravenh.

Boulenger, Ind. Rept. p. 456; W. Sclater, P. Z. S. 1892, p. 345.
Distribution—Ceylon.

| 1 Ceylon | E. F. Kelaart, A. S. B. | 10037. |
| | (TYPE OF LYMNODYTES MACULARIA, Bly.) | |

27. RANA MALABARICA, Dum. & Bibr.

Boulenger, Ind. Rept. p. 456.
Distribution—Hills of South-west India from Matheran downwards.

1 Nadowli, Western Ghats	F. Stoliczka	2731.
1 South Canara	Col. R. H. Beddome	2833.
2 Malabar	E. Gerard [P.]	12494, 12499.
1 Cochin	F. Stoliczka	4072.

28. RANA CURTIPES, Jerdon.

Boulenger, Ind. Rept. p. 458.
Distribution—South-western India, from Mysore to Malabar.

1 Koppa, Mysore	W. M. Daly	13564.
1 Wynaad	Col. R. H. Beddome	9430.
1 Malabar	E. Gerard [P.]	12512.

29. RANA NIGROVITTATA (Blyth).

Limnodytes nigrovittatus, Blyth, J. A. S. B. xxiv. 1855, p. 718.
Rana tytleri, Theobald, Boulenger, Ind. Rept. p. 458.
Rana nigrovittata, W. Sclater, P. Z. S. 1892, p. 345.

Distribution—Throughout Assam and Burma.

7	Khasia hills	Dr. T. C. Jerdon	10039–45.
		(TYPICAL OF R. PIPIENS, Jerdon.)	
24	Cherrapunji	J. H. Bourne	10441–64.
1	Tezpur	Dulila Exped. (Godwin-Austen)	3963.
1	Sibsagar	S. E. Peal	4009.
3	Samagooting	Capt. J. Butler	10197 9.
1	Dilcosh, Cachar	J. Inglis	11370.
3	Pegu	F. Stoliczka	3574–5, 10816.
4	Moulmein	F. Stoliczka	2758, 3571–3.
7	Meetan, 3500 feet	Tenasserim Exped. (Limborg)	9526–32.
3	Hatsiga	Tenasserim Exped. (Limborg)	9523–5.
9	Ahsoon	Tenasserim Exped. (Limborg)	4844–6, 9544–9.
15	Between Ahsoon and Meetan	Tenasserim Exped. (Limborg)	10473–87.
3	Mergui	W. Theobald, A. S. B.	2685, 2773–4.
		(TYPES OF THE SPECIES, Bly.)	

30. RANA GRANULOSA, Anders.

Anderson, J. A. S. B. xl. 1871, p. 23; W. Sclater, P. Z. S. 1892, p. 346.

Distribution—Assam, Pegu, and Tenasserim.

1	Sibsagar	S. E. Peal	2789.
1	Pegu	W. Theobald	2780.
		(CO-TYPES OF R. GRANULOSA, Anders.)	
2	Sibsagar	S. E. Peal	9440, 10830.
7	Mooleyit Mt. 3500–6000 ft.	Tenasserim Exped. (Limborg)	4098, 8974–6.

31. RANA NICOBARIENSIS (Stol.).

Boulenger, Ind. Rept. p. 459.
Distribution—Nicobars and Nias Isles, Sumatra.

14	Nicobars	F. Stoliczka	2782–6, 3562–70.
		(TYPES OF THE SPECIES, Stol.)	

32. RANA TEMPORALIS (Günth.).

Boulenger, Ind. Rept. p. 459.
Distribution—Hills of Southern India and Ceylon.

1	Shevaroy hills, Salem dist.	W. L. Sclater	13545.
4	Conoor, Nilgiris	Dr. F. Day	4298–4301.
1	Conoor, Nilgiris	Col. R. H. Beddome [Ex.]	10248.
3	Malabar	Dr. T. C. Jerdon	2776–8.
		(TYPICAL OF RANA FLAVESCENS, Jerdon.	

2 Malabar	E. Gerard [P.]	12500-1.
18 South India	Col. R. H. Beddome	10583, 10586, 10589, 10593,
		10596-7,10601,10618, 10625,
		10643, 10654, 10663, 10690,
		10702, 10711, 10720,
		10722, 10737.
1 Ceylon	No history	10038.

33. RANA ERYTHRÆA (Schleg.).

Boulenger, Ind. Rept. p. 460; W. Sclater, P. Z. S. 1892, p. 345.
Distribution—Lower Bengal, Assam, S. Burma.

1 Calcutta	F. Stoliczka	2684.
1 Dacca	Col. Tytler, A. S. B.	10035.
	(TYPE OF R. TYTLERI, Theobald.)	
1 Garo hills	Col. H. H. Godwin-Austen	2709.
4 Shway-goo-myo	Yunan Exped., 1875 (Anderson)	9403-6.
2 Pegu	W. Theobald, A. S. B.	10033-4.
1 Taoo	Tenasserim Exped. (Limborg)	4841.
2 Taing, King Isle	Mergui Exped. (Anderson)	11844, 11846.

34. RANA MONTICOLA (Anders.).

Boulenger, Ind. Rept. p. 461.
Distribution—Sikkim Himalayas extending to Assam.

1 Darjeeling	J. Gammie	10036.
	(TYPE OF THE SPECIES, Anders.)	
1 Darjeeling	J. Gammie	10781.
1 Darjeeling	Capt. Jerdan	10959.
1 Nanki R., Assam?	S. E. Peal	3855.
2 No loc.	No hist.	10944-5.

35. RANA LIVIDA (Blyth).

Boulenger, Ind. Rept. p. 462.
Distribution—Sikkim, Assam, Tenasserim, and Hongkong.

2 Darjeeling	J. Gammie	10364-5.
2 Khasia hills	No history	10190-1.
11 Cherrapunji	J. H. Bourne	9780, 9787, 9798,
		9801-2, 9812-4, 9833-5.
8 Tenasserim	W. Theobald, A. S. B.	10182-9.
2 No history	A. S. B.	10180-1.

36. RANA LATOPALMATA, Boul.

Boulenger, Ind. Rept. p. 462.
Distribution—Sikkim, Assam, Burma, and Yunan.

| 9 Darjeeling | J. Gammie | 10120-1, 10124, 10765, |
| | | 10767-8, 10770-1, 10774. |

1 Khasia hills	Dr. T. C. Jerdon	10174.
1 Khasia hills	Col. H. H. Godwin-Austen	10168.
1 Cherrapunji	Col. H. H. Godwin-Austen	2714.
18 Cherrapunji	J. H. Bourne	10072-4, 10081-2, 10084, 10087, 10091, 10095-6, 10099-100, 10102, 10104, 10106, 10110, 10116, 10119.
1 Hotha	Yunan Exped. (Anderson)	4167.
4 Pegu	Major Berdmore, A. S. B.	10202-5.
1 No loc.	No history	10328.

37. RANA HIMALAYANA, Boul.

Boulenger, Ind. Rept. p. 463.
Distribution—Himalayas from Simla to Darjeeling.

1 Simla	A. Newnham	13587.

38. RANA GLANDULOSA, Boul.

Boulenger, Cat. Batr. Sal. p. 73, pl. vii.
Distribution—The Malay Peninsula and Borneo.

2 Malacca	Raffles Mus. (Davison)	13317-8.

39. RANA DELALANDII (Tschudi).

Boulenger, Cat. Batr. Sal. p. 31.
Distribution—South and East Africa.

1 No loc.	No hist., A. S. B.	9616.

40. RANA RUGOSA, Schleg.

Boulenger, Cat. Batr. Sal. p. 35.
Distribution—Japan.

1 Mino, Osaka	J. Anderson	13003.
4 Lake Chimjiji	J. Anderson	12998-13001.
3 Enoshina	J. Anderson	13009-11.

41. RANA CATESBIANA, Shaw.

Boulenger, Cat. Batr. Sal. p. 36.
Distribution—North-east America.

6 Lucknow, Ontario	J. H. Garnier [Ex.]	12121-5, 12135 8.
1 Blackhorse Lake, Ont.	J. H. Garnier [Ex.]	12183.
2 Lake Ontario (larvæ)	J. H. Garnier [Ex.]	12121-2.
4 Ontario	J. H. Garnier [Ex.]	12216 9.
3 Ontario (larvæ)	J. H. Garnier [Ex.]	12212 4.

42. RANA CLAMATA, Daud.

Boulenger, Cat. Batr. Sal. p. 36.
Distribution—Eastern North America.

2 Ontario (juv. et larva)	J. H. Garnier	12123, 12100.

43. RANA SEPTENTRIONALIS, Baird.

Boulenger, Cat. Batr. Sal. p. 37.
Distribution—Canada to Montana.

1 Lucknow, Ontario	J. H. Garnier	12215.

44. RANA ESCULENTA, Linn.

Boulenger, Cat. Batr. Sal. p. 38.
Distribution—Europe, Western Asia, and North Africa.

1 France	M. Malherbe, A. S. B.	9104.
5 Berlin	G. A. Boulenger	13858-62.
2 Imole, Lombardy	Prof. Cornalia [Ex.]	9428-9.
5 Lombardy	Prof. Cornalia [Ex.]	9378-80, 9438-9.
1 Europe	Hungarian Mus., A. S. B.	9103.
1 Baalbek, Cœlesyria	J. Anderson	11211.
11 Damascus	J. Anderson	11198-11200, 11202-4, 11334-8.
1 Mt. Hermon	J. Anderson	11207.
1 Upper Jordan valley	J. Anderson	11195.
4 Sea of Galilee	J. Anderson	11196-7, 11344-5.
2 The Herith, Plains of Jericho	J. Anderson	11340, 11342.
1 Resht, Caspian Sea	Persian Coll.	3526.
11 Shiraz, Persia	Mus. Coll.	9108-12, 9114-9.
1 nr. Shiraz	Persian Coll.	3527.
1 Basreh, Persian Gulf	Persian Coll.	3528.

Subsp. japonica.

Boulenger, Cat. Batr. Sal. p. 40.
Distribution—China and Japan.

1 Gokbaibe, Japan	J. Anderson	13007.
8 Central Japan	J. Anderson	13021-8.

45. RANA UTRICULARIA, Harlan.

Boulenger, Cat. Batr. Sal. p. 40.
Distribution—United States.

3 Texas	Dr. J. H. Garnier [Ex.]	12134, 12139, 12184.

46. RANA HALECINA, Kalm.

Boulenger, Cat. Batr. Sal. p. 41.
Distribution—North and Central America.

1 Carberry. Manitoba	Dr. J. H. Garnier [Ex.]	12774.
9 Ontario	Dr. J. H. Garnier [Ex.]	12129-31, 12141, 12146,
		12189, 12202-4.
3 Ontario (larvæ)	Dr. J. H. Garnier [Ex.]	12193.
1 Guatemala	E. Gerard [P.]	12506.

47. RANA PALUSTRIS, Leconte.

Boulenger, Cat. Batr. Sal. p. 42.
Distribution—United States.

1 Lucknow, Ontario	Dr. J. H. Garnier [Ex.]	12301.
1 Ontario	Dr. J. H. Garnier [Ex.]	12220-1.

48. RANA TEMPORARIA, Linn.

Boulenger. Cat. Batr. Sal. p. 44.
Distribution—Europe and Northern Asia to Japan.

2 England	R. Hancock, A. S. B.	9106-7.
1 Tyrol	G. A. Boulenger	13057.
8 Yezo, Japan	J. Anderson	13013 20.

Subsp. parvapalmata.

1 Galicia	G. A. Boulenger	13067.

49. RANA ARVALIS, Nilsson.

Boulenger, Cat. Batr. Sal. p. 45.
Distribution—Eastern Europe and Western Asia.

3 Breslau	G. A. Boulenger	13063 5.

50. RANA AGILIS, Thomas.

Boulenger, Cat. Batr. Sal. p. 46.
Distribution—France, N. Italy, Austria, and Greece.

1 Brittany	G. A. Boulenger	13066.

51. RANA SILVATICA, Leconte.

Boulenger, Cat. Batr. Sal. p. 47.
Distribution—N. America.

2 Brit. Columbia	Dr. J. H. Garnier [Ex.]	12132-3.
1 Lucknow, Ontario	Dr. J. H. Garnier [Ex.]	12295.
4 Ontario	Dr. J. H. Garnier [Ex.]	12210-1, 12338-9.

52. RANA OXYRHYNCHUS (Sundev.).

Boulenger, Cat. Batr. Sal. p. 51.
Distribution—South and West Africa.

| 1 Madagascar ? | E. Gerard [P.] | 12520. |

53. RANA MASCARENIENSIS, Dum. & Bibr.

Boulenger, Cat. Batr. Sal. p. 52.
Distribution—Africa.

| 2 Lebka, Abyssinia | W. T. Blanford | 2733-4. |

54. RANA INGUINALIS, Günth.

Boulenger, Cat. Batr. Sal. p. 67.
Distribution—Madagascar.

| 1 Madagascar | E. Gerard [P.] | 12495. |

55. RANA COWANII, Boul.

Boulenger, Cat. Batr. Sal. p. 463.
Distribution—Madagascar.

| 1 Betsileo, Madagascar | E. Gerard [P.] | 12532. |

56. RANA BUERGERI (Schleg.).

Boulenger, Cat. Batr. Sal. p. 73.
Distribution—Japan.

| 1 Mino, Osaka, Japan | J. Anderson | 13003. |

57. MICRIXALUS SAXICOLA (Jerdon).

Boulenger, Ind. Rept. p. 465.
Distribution—Malabar and the Wynaad.

| 15 South India | Col. R. H. Beddome | 10590-1, 10604, 10607, 10617, 10629, 10653, 10664, 10672-3, 10704, 10710, 10717-8, 10749. |

58. MICRIXALUS FUSCUS (Boul.).

Boulenger, Ind. Rept. p. 466.
Distribution—Hills of Southern India.

1 Anamalai hills	E. Gerard [P.]	12537.
11 Travancore	Col. R. H. Beddome	2823-7, 4318 23.
4 Tinnevelli hills	Col. R. H. Beddome	10249-52.
22 South India	Col. R. H. Beddome	10602, 10609, 10612, 10619, 10633, 10655, 10671, 10677, 10691, 10694 5, 10715, 10721, 10729, 10736, 10738-9, 10746, 10750-1, 10755, 10761.

59. MICRIXALUS SILVATICUS (Boul.).

Boulenger, Ind. Rept. p. 466.
Distribution—Malabar.

9 South India	Col. R. H. Beddome	10628, 10634, 10640, 10649, 10688, 10716, 10726, 10742, 10759.
3 No. loc.	No hist., A. S. B.	10934, 10936, 10938.

60. NYCTIBATRACHUS MAJOR, Boul.

Boulenger, Ind. Rept. p. 468.
Distribution—South-west India from the Wynaad to Travancore.

2 Wynaad	T. C. Jerdon	2737-8.
1 Travancore	Col. R. H. Beddome	2835.
2 South India	Col. R. H. Beddome	10610, 10612.
1 South India	E. Gerard [P.]	12535.

61. NANNOBATRACHUS BEDDOMII, Boul.

Boulenger, Ind. Rept. p. 468.
Distribution—Hills of South India.

1 Anamalai hills	Col. R. H. Beddome	10970.
1 Tinnevelli	E. Gerrard [P.]	12538.
3 South India	Col. R. H. Beddome	10703, 10709, 10732.

62. RHACOPHORUS MAXIMUS, Günth.

Boulenger, Ind. Rept. p. 472.
Distribution—Sikkim and Assam hills.

2 Cherrapunji, Assam	J. H. Bourne	9518-9.
1 Khasia hills	Dr. T. C. Jerdon	10300.
1 Jyntea hills	Col. H. H. Godwin-Austen	10290.

13 Sibsagar dist.	S. E. Peal	10268 73, 10276 81
		10307.
8 Samagooting	Capt. J. Butler	11258 9, 11261 4.
		11266 7.
4 Naga hills	Owen	10282 5.

63. RHACOPHORUS BIMACULATUS, Boul.

Boulenger, Ind. Rept. p. 472.
Distribution—Assam hills.

| 4 Cherrapunji, Assam | J. H. Bourne | 10286 9. |
| 1 Khasia hills | Col. H. H. Godwin-Austen | 10291. |

(TYPE OF R. MACULATUS, Anders.; name changed by Boulenger.)

| 4 Khasia hills | Dr. T. C. Jerdon | 2753-6. |
| 1 Samagooting | Capt. J. Butler | 2760. |

64. RHACOPHORUS MALABARICUS, Jerdon.

Boulenger, Ind. Rept. p. 473.
Distribution—Malabar and Travancore.

| 1 Trevandrum | H. Ferguson | 13581. |

65. RHACOPHORUS BEDDOMII, Boul.

Boulenger, Ind. Rept. p. 473.
Distribution—Tinnevelli dist., S. India.

| 1 Tinnevelli | E. Gerard [P.] | 12497. |

66. RHACOPHORUS LATERALIS, Boul.

Boulenger, Ind. Rept. p. 473; W. Sclater, P. Z. S. 1892, p. 346.
Distribution—Mysore and Malabar.

| 1 Koppa, Mysore | W. M. Daly | 13565. |

67. RHACOPHORUS TUBERCULATUS (Anders.).

Boulenger, Ind. Rept. p. 474.
Distribution—Assam.

| 5 Sibsagar, Assam | S. E. Peal | 10152-6. |

(TYPES OF THE SPECIES, Anders.).

68. RHACOPHORUS LEUCOMYSTAX (Gravenh.).

Boulenger, Ind. Rept. p. 474.
Distribution—Sikkim, Assam, Burma, Southern China. Malay
Peninsula and Islands.

8 Darjeeling	J. Gammie	10126-9, 10149-51, 10165.
1 Lingling, Kurseong	T. Johnston	10194.
1 Jessore	W. R. G. Frith, A. S. B.	10051.
1 Dacca	Col. R. C. Tytler, A. S. B.	10053.
1 Cherrapunji, Assam	J. H. Bourne	9783.
1 Gauhati	Mus. Coll.	10130.
5 Goalpara	H. L. Haughton	9482-3, 10143-5.
7 Sibsagar dist.	S. E. Peal	10175, 10231, 10424-8.
13 Samagooting	Capt. J. Butler	10131-42, 10230.
1 Dilcosh, N.E. Cachar	J. Inglis	11369.
1 Cachar	Mus. Coll.	2781.
3 Sylhet	F. Skipwith, A. S. B.	10052-4.
1 Pegu	E. Gerard [P.]	12503.
3 Pegu	W. Theobald	10060, 10166-7.
1 Meeta, Tenesserim	Tenasserim Exped. (Limborg)	10195.
1 Lampee, Mergui	Mergui Exped. (Anderson)	11852.
1 Tiboo Padaw, Mergui	Mergui Exped. (Aederson)	11851.
2 Penang	F. Stoliczka	3587-8.
5 Perak (Larut)	J. Anderson	13171-5.
1 Malay Peninsula	Raffles Mus. (Davison)	13344.
3 Hongkong	J. Wood-Mason	13252-5.

69. RHACOPHORUS MACULATUS (Gray).

Boulenger, Ind. Rept. p. 475.

Distribution—Throughout India to Ceylon, extending eastwards to Calcutta.

1 Allahabad	J. Cockburn	10242.
5 Chanda, C. P.	Mus. Coll.	10160-4.
3 E. of Chanda	W. T. Blanford	10146-8.
1 Upper Godavery dist., C. P.	Dr. Goffney	2762.
1 Malabar	E. Gerard [P.]	12510.
1 Anamalai hills	Col. R. H. Beddome	2828.
4 Travancore	Col. R. H. Beddome	2821-2, 2836-7.
1 Trevandrum, Travancore	H. Ferguson	
2 S. India	Col. R. H. Beddome	10584, 10599.
2 Ceylon	E. F. Kelaart, A. S. B.	10055-6.
1 Ceylon	E. Gerard [P.]	12522.
1 Chaibassa, Singbhhoom	H. L. Haughton, A. S. B.	10057.
1 Singhbhoom	V. Ball	10169.
1 Chota Nagpur	V. Ball	10239.
1 Raneegunge	Mus. Coll.	2757.
11 Calcutta	E. Blyth, A. S. B.	10061-71.
1 Alipore, Calcutta	V. Ball	10173.
1 Alipore, Calcutta	J. Cockburn	10241.
1 Alipore, Calcutta	Babu R. B. Sannyal	11468.
Tadpoles, Zoological Gardens	J. Anderson	12607-10.
1 Botanical Gardens	J. Anderson	10059.
1 Botanical Gardens	G. Nevill	2707.

70. RHACOPHORUS CRUCIGER (Blyth).

Boulenger, Ind. Rept. p. 476.
Distribution—Ceylon.

4 Ceylon	E. F. Kelaart, A. S. B.	10176-9.
	(TYPES OF THE SPECIES, Bly.)	
2 Ceylon	H. Nevill	10789-90.
1 Colombo	W. Ferguson	10016.

71. RHACOPHORUS EQUES (Günth.).

Boulenger, Ind. Rept. p. 476.
Distribution—Ceylon.

1 Ceylon	E. Gerard [P.]	12517.

72. RHACOPHORUS NANUS (Günth.).

Boulenger, Ind. Rept. p. 478.
Distribution—Ceylon and South India?

1 S. India?	E. Gerard [P.]	12493.

73. RHACOPHORUS PLEUROSTICTUS (Günth.).

Boulenger, Ind. Rept. p. 479.
Distribution—Hills of Southern India.

2 Nilgiri hills	Dr. T. C. Jerdon	10157-9.
1 Nilgiri hills	E. Gerard [P.]	12513.
1 Madras Pr.	W. Davison	9550.
5 South India	Col. R. H. Beddome	10214, 10582, 10600, 10632, 10684.

74. RHACOPHORUS MICROTYMPANUM (Günth.).

Boulenger, Ind. Rept. p. 479.
Distribution—Ceylon.

7 Ceylon	H. Nevill	10791-2, 10794, 10798, 10800-2.

75. RHACOPHORUS STICTOMERUS (Günth.).

Boulenger, Ind. Rept. p. 480.
Distribution—Ceylon.

1 Ceylon	R. C. Morgan	10946.

76. RHACOPHORUS CAVIROSTRIS (Günth.).

Boulenger, Ind. Rept. p. 481 : W. Sclater, P. Z. S. 1892, p. 346.
Distribution—Ceylon and Tenasserim.

| 1 Tenasserim | Tenasserim Exped. (Lim-borg) | 10964. |

77. RHACOPHORUS GOUDOTI (Tschudi).

Boulenger, Cat. Batr. Sal. p. 76.
Distribution—Madagascar.

| 1 Madagascar | E. Gerard [P.] | 12496. |

78. RHACOPHORUS SCHLEGELII (Günth.).

Boulenger, Cat. Batr. Sal. p. 86.
Distribution—Japan.

| 1 Enoshima, Japan | J. Anderson | 13008. |

79. IXALUS OXYRHYNCHUS, Günth.

Boulenger, Ind. Rept. p. 482.
Distribution—Ceylon and South India ?

| 1 South India | Col. R. H. Beddome | 10730. |

80. IXALUS LEUCORHINUS, Martens.

Boulenger, Ind. Rept. p. 483.
Distribution—Malabar and Ceylon.

| 1 South India | Col. R. H. Beddome | 10642. |

81. IXALUS NASUTUS, Günth.

Boulenger, Ind. Rept. p. 484.
Distribution—Ceylon and South India.

| 17 South India | Col. R. H. Beddome | 10592, 10615, 10620, 10624, 10641, 10661, 10665, 10669, 10680, 10687, 10693-4, 10698, 10701, 10734, 10741, 10752. |
| 5 Ceylon | H. Nevill | 10793, 10795-7, 10799. |

c 2

82. IXALUS CINERASCENS, Stol.

Stoliczka, Proc. A. S. B. 1870, p. 275; W. Sclater, P. Z. S. 1892, p. 347.
Distribution—Burma.

1 Moulmein	F. Stoliczka	2716.
	(Type of the species, Stol.)	

83. IXALUS PULCHER, Boul.

Boulenger, Ind. Rept. p. 485.
Distribution—Wynaad, South India.

1 Manatoddy, Wynaad	E. Gerard [P.]	12531.

84. IXALUS VARIABILIS, Günth.

Boulenger, Ind. Rept. p. 487.
Distribution—Throughout Southern India and Ceylon, from the Vizagapatam district southwards.

7 Golconda hills, Vizag. district	Col. R. H. Beddome	2868-74.
4 Anamalai hills	Col. R. II. Beddome	2829-32.
1 Malabar	E. Gerard [P.]	12504.
1 Travancore	Col. R. II. Beddome	2843.
4 Tinnevelli	Col. R. H. Beddome [Ex.]	9407-10.
17 S. India	Col. R. II. Beddome	10648, 10650, 10657, 10676, 10678-9, 10682, 10224, 10226, 10228, 10568, 10659-60, 10706, 10740, 10747, 10754.
4 Ceylon	O. Morgan	10953-6.
1 No loc.	No history, A. S. B.	10937.

85. IXALUS SIGNATUS, Boul.

Boulenger, Ind. Rept. p. 487.
Distribution—Malabar dist., South India.

4 South India	Col. R. II. Beddome	10603, 10605, 10714, 10723.

86. IXALUS FLAVIVENTRIS, Boul.

Boulenger, Ind. Rept. 487.
Distribution—Malabar dist., South India.

1 South India	Col. R. II. Beddome	10588.

87. IXALUS CHALAZODES, Günth.

Boulenger, Ind. Rept. p. 488.
Distribution—Travancore.

| 1 S. India | Col. R. H. Beddome | 10636. |

88. IXALUS GLANDULOSUS (Jerdon).

Boulenger, Ind. Rept. p. 488 ; W. Sclater, P. Z. S. 1892, p. 347.
Distribution—Hills of South India.

1 Nilgiri hills	W. Theobald	2709.
	(TYPE OF I. PUNCTATUS, Theobald.)	
1 Malabar	E. Gerard [P.].	12529.
14 S. India	Col. R. H. Beddome	10215-7, 10219,
		10221-3, 10227,
		10229, 10567, 10606,
		10613-4, 10662.

89. IXALUS ASPER (Boul.).

Boulenger, P. Z. S. 1886, p. 415 ; W. Sclater, P. Z. S. 1892, p. 347.
Distribution—Hills of Burma and the Malay Peninsula.

| 1 Burma-Siam hills | Mus. Collector | 12792. |

Family DENDROBATIDÆ.

90. DENDROBATES TINCTORIUS (Schneid.).

Boulenger, Cat. Batr. Sal. p. 142.
Distribution—Tropical America.

| 1 Ecuador | E. Gerard [P.] | 12527. |

Family ENGYSTOMATIDÆ.

91. PHRYNISCUS LÆVIS, Günth.

Boulenger, Cat. Batr. Sal. p. 151.
Distribution—Western Neotropical Region.

| 1 Ecuador | E. Gerard [P.] | 12525. |

92. PHRYNISCUS VARIUS (Stannius).

Boulenger, Cat. Batr. Sal. p. 152.
Distribution—Central America and Northern South America.

| 2 Costa Rica | E. Gerard [P.] | 12539-40. |

93. MELANOBATRACHUS INDICUS, Bedd.

Boulenger, Ind. Rept. p. 489.
Distribution—Hills of S. India.

1 Anamalai hills	Col. R. H. Beddome	10969.
1 Travancore	E. Gerard [P.]	12530.

94. CALOPHRYNUS PLEUROSTIGMA, Tschudi.

Boulenger, Ind. Rept. p. 490.
Distribution—Burma, South China, and Borneo.

1 Pegu	W. Theobald, A. S. B.	9853.
	(Type of Engystoma interlineatum, Bly. ?)	
3 Ahsoon, Tenasserim	Tenasserim Exped. (Limborg)	9841-3.
1 No loc.	W. Theobald	2694.

95. MICROHYLA RUBRA (Jerdon).

Boulenger, Ind. Rept. p. 491.
Distribution—Assam, South India, and Ceylon.

2 Nellore	Dr. T. C. Jerdon	9838-9.
1 Malabar	E. Gerard [P.]	12534.
1 South India	W. Theobald	2680.
1 South India	Col. R. H. Beddome	10566.
1 No loc.	No hist., A. S. B.	2713.

96. MICROHYLA ORNATA (Dum. & Bibr.).

Boulenger, Ind. Rept. p. 491.
Distribution—Throughout the Indian Empire from Kashmir to Ceylon, extending eastwards to Assam, Burma, S. China, and Indo-China.

1 Timali, Kashmir	Yarkand Exped. (Stoliczka)	10243.
2 nr. Ellore	W. T. Blanford	2728-9.
2 Collagelly hills	Col. R. H. Beddome	10929-30.
1 Tinnevelli hills	E. Gerard [P.]	12526.
8 Paresnath, Manbhum dist.	F. Stoliczka [Ex.]	2765-72.
9 Beerbhoom	W. Theobald, A. S. B.	2739-47.
2 Dacca	Col. R. C. Tytler, A. S. B.	2735-6.
1 Cherrapunji	J. H. Bourne	10438.
2 Goalpara, Assam	H. L. Haughton	2710-1.
1 Nampoung, Kakhyen hills	Yunan Exped. (Anderson)	9521.
2 Tsitkaw, Upper Burma	Yunan Exped. (Anderson)	9522, 10933.
1 Pegu	W. Theobald	2730.
2 Moulmein	F. Stoliczka	3582-3.
1 Martaban	F. Stoliczka	2706.
2 Ahsoon, Tenasserim	Tenasserim Exped. (Limborg)	4847-8.
2 Tenasserim	Tenasserim Exped. (Limborg)	10940-1.
3 Tavoy	Mergui Exped. (Anderson)	11847-9.

3 Zadiwoon mangrove swamp	Mergui Exped. (Anderson)	11853–5.
1 Mithanthoung	Mergui Exped. (Anderson)	11843.
6 No loc.	W. Theobald	2688–93.

97. MICROHYLA ACHATINA (Boie).

Boulenger, Cat. Batr. Sal. p. 166; W. Sclater, P. Z. S. 1892, p. 347.
Distribution—Tenasserim, Java, and the Moluccas.

| 1 Ahsoon, Tenasserim | Tenasserim Exped. (Limborg) | 5876. |

98. MICROHYLA BERDMORII (Blyth).

Boulenger, Ind. Rept. p. 492.
Distribution—Burma, extending southwards to Malay Peninsula.

3 Arakan	Sir A. Phayre	9718–20.
	(TYPES OF THE SPECIES, Bly.)	
1 Malacca	Raffles Museum (Davison)	13351.

99. CALLULA OBSCURA, Günth.

Boulenger, Ind. Rept. p. 493.
Distribution—Southern India and Ceylon.

| 1 South India | Col. R. H. Beddome | 12508. |

100. CALLULA PULCHRA, Gray.

Boulenger, Ind. Rept. p. 494.
Distribution—India and Ceylon, Burma, Southern China, Indo-China, and the Malay Peninsula.

2 Botanical Gardens, Calcutta	J. Anderson	10362–3.
1 Mandalay	Yunan Exped. (Anderson)	10360.
3 Ava	Yunan Exped. (Anderson)	9484–6.
1 Moulmein	Capt. Hood	10943.
2 Moulmein	F. Stoliczka	3584, 10359.
1 Tavoy	Mus. Coll.	12837.
1 Burma	C. S. Bligh	10361.
1 Malay Peninsula	Raffles Mus. (Davison)	13315.
7 No loc.	Dr. T. C. Jerdon	10351–3, 10355–8.

101. CALLULA VARIEGATA, Stol.

Boulenger, Ind. Rept. p. 494.
Distribution—Southern India, from Ellore southwards, and Ceylon.

1 Ellore	W. T. Blanford	2761.
	(TYPE OF THE SPECIES, Stol.)	
1 Anamalai hills	E. Gerard [P.]	12524.

102. CALLULA TRIANGULARIS, Günth.

Boulenger, Ind. Rept. p. 495.
Distribution—Nilgiri hills and Malabar.

| 1 Nilgiri hills | Col. R. H. Beddome | 2818. |
| 1 Nilgiri hills | E. Gerard [P.] | 12521. |

103. CACOPUS SYSTOMA (Schneid.).

Boulenger, Ind. Rept. p. 496.
Distribution—Throughout India, from the North-west Provinces southwards.

6 Agra	Agra Mus.	9642–7.
3 Allahabad	J. Cockburn	9490–2.
2 Collagelly hills	Col. R. H. Beddome	9618–9.
1 Travancore	Col. R. H. Beddome	2834.
1 No loc.	No hist., A. S. B.	2727.

104. CACOPUS GLOBULOSUS, Günth.

Boulenger, Ind. Rept. p. 497.
Distribution—India, recorded from Bengal, Ganjam, and Berar.

1 South Berar	J. Anderson	2749.
1 Botanical Gardens, Cal-		
cutta	J. Anderson	9678.
1 No loc.	No history	9680.

Family CYSTIGNATHIDÆ.

105. HYLODES CONSPICILLATUS (Cope).

Boulenger, Cat. Batr. Sal. p. 204.
Distribution—Ecuador.

| 1 Ecuador | E. Gerard [P.] | 12502. |

106. HYLODES LINEATUS (Schneid.).

Boulenger, Cat. Batr. Sal. p. 207.
Distribution—Northern Neotropical region.

| 1 "Piatanger" | E. Gerard [P.] | 12528. |

107. EDALORHINA PEREZII, Espada.

Boulenger, Cat. Batr. Sal. p. 227.
Distribution—Ecuador.

1 Ecuador	E. Gerard [P.]	12505.

108. PALUDICOLA BIBRONII (Tschudi).

Boulenger, Cat. Batr. Sal. p. 231.
Distribution—South America.

1 Chili	E. Gerard [P.]	12533.

109. LIMNODYNASTES TASMANIENSIS, Steindachn.

Boulenger, Cat. Batr. Sal. p. 260.
Distribution—Australia and Tasmania.

1 Sydney, N.S.W.	G. Nevill	12871-2.
1 Australia	No history	11910.

110. HYPEROLIA MARMORATA, Gray.

Boulenger, Cat. Batr. Sal. p. 267.
Distribution—Australia.

1 Paramatta, N.S.W.	E. Gerard [P.]	12490.

Family BUFONIDÆ.

111. PSEUDOPHRYNE AUSTRALIS (Gray).

Boulenger, Cat. Batr. Sal. p. 277.
Distribution—Australia.

1 Australia	No history	12511.

112. BUFO KELAARTII, Günth.

Boulenger, Ind. Rept. p. 502.
Distribution—Ceylon.

1 Ceylon	H. Nevill	10788.

113. BUFO LATASTII, Boul.

Boulenger, Ind. Rept. p. 503.
Distribution—Ladak in Kashmir.

1 Kashmir	Yarkand Exped. (Stoliczka)	10247.
1 Kashmir	T. C. Jerdon	9856.

114. BUFO VIRIDIS, Laur.

Boulenger, Ind. Rept. p. 504.
Distribution—Europe east of the Rhine and Rhone, N. Africa,
Western and Central Asia, extending to Kashmir and the Himalayas.

1 Dresden	G. A. Boulenger	13068.
2 Lombardy	Prof. Cornalia	9377, 9498.
6 Damascus	J. Anderson	11205, 11328–32.
2 Base of Mt. Tabor, Galilee	J. Anderson	11208–9.
2 Jerusalem	J. Anderson	11192–3.
7 Plains of Jericho	J. Anderson	11213–4, 11216–9, 11339.
1 Ghilan, Persia	W. T. Blanford	3511.
6 Shiraz, Persia	Museum Coll.	9141–6.
4 Bushire, Persia	W. D. Cumming	13463–6.
3 Berar, S.E. Persia	W. T. Blanford	3508–9, 9951.
1 Karman, S.E. Persia	W. T. Blanford	3512.
9 Tirphul, Afghanistan	Afghan Bound. Comm.	13114–22.
1 Dizak, Baluchistan	W. T. Blanford	3510.
9 Kashgar	Yarkand Exped. (Stoliczka)	9391–8, 10240.
4 Yangihissar	Yarkand Exped. (Stoliczka)	9475–8.
8 Yarkand	Yarkand Exped. (Stoliczka)	9467–74.
4 Yarkand	Hon. C. Ellis	12583–6.
1 Eastern Turkestan	J. Scully	13200.
1 Zunj, nr. Wakkan, Pamir	Yarkand Exped. (Stoliczka)	10632.
2 Chitral	G. M. Giles.	13078–9.
7 Ladak	Museum Coll.	9682–8.
3 Kashmir	Yarkand Exped. (Stoliczka)	10244–6.

115. BUFO ANDERSONII, Boul.

Boulenger, Ind. Rept. p. 504.
Distribution -The Himalayas and North-western India, extending
westwards to Muscat and Arabia.

2 Simla	F. Stoliczka	2763–4.
6 Shahpur, Punjab	G. Henderson	13256–61.
1 Lower Sind	F. Fedden	10976.
22 Agra	Agra Museum	9868, 9871, 9954–61, 10017–28.
1 Allahabad, N. W. P.	J. Cockburn	9499.
3 Purneah	Museum Collector	9689–91.

116. BUFO OLIVACEUS, Blanf.

Boulenger, Ind. Rept. p. 504.
Distribution—Baluchistan.

1 Dasht R., Baluchistan	W. T. Blanford	3523.
1 Ghistigan, Baluchistan	W. T. Blanford	3524.
1 Bahu Kelat, Baluchistan	W. T. Blanford	3525.

(3 CO-TYPES OF THE SPECIES, Blanf.)

117. BUFO STOMATICUS, Lütken.

Boulenger, Ann. Mag. N. H. (6) vii. 1891, p. 463; W. Sclater,
P. Z. S. 1892, p. 347.
Distribution—Bengal, Assam, and Burma.

1 Bowanipur, Calcutta	Pundit Pramanath	10968.
2 Burma	J. Wood-Mason	8979-80.
1 No loc.	No history	10827.

118. BUFO HIMALAYANUS, Günth.

Boulenger, Ind. Rept. p. 505.
Distribution—The Himalayas from Simla to Sikkim.

2 Kotagherry, nr. Simla	F. Stoliczka	9952-3.
2 Simla	A. Newnham	13588-9.
1 Tamlong, Sikkim	W. T. Blanford	9983.
1 Sikkim, 5000 ft.	W. T. Blanford	10031.
2 No loc.	Museum Coll., 1869	10498-9.

119. BUFO MICROTYMPANUM, Boul.

Boulenger, Ind. Rept. p. 505.
Distribution—Southern India, Malabar, and the Nilgiris.

| 3 Nilgiris | T. C. Jerdon | 9937-8. |

120. BUFO PENANGENSIS (Stol.).

Boulenger, Cat. Batr. Sal. p. 287.
Distribution—Penang.

| 2 Penang | F. Stoliczka | 3585-6. |

(TYPES OF THE SPECIES, Stol.?)

121. BUFO MELANOSTICTUS, Schneid.

Boulenger, Ind. Rept. p. 505.
Distribution—Throughout the Indian Empire from the Himalayas
to Ceylon, extending eastwards to S. China, the Malay Peninsula and
Archipelago.

4 Katmandu, Nepal	Museum Coll.	9998-10001.
2 Mt. Aboo, Rjpt.	Dr. G. S. Sutherland	9935-6.
1 Agra	Agra Museum [Ex.]	9844.
1 Allahabad	J. Cockburn	10012.
1 Chanda, C. P.	Museum Coll.	2817.
1 High Range, Travancore	H. Ferguson	13582.
12 South India	Col. R. H. Beddome	10569-72, 10574-81.
2 Colombo	J. Anderson	10002-3.
5 Ceylon	E. F. Kelaart, A. S. B.	9845-9.
1 Ceylon	C. Morgan	10948.
1 Ceylon	J. Anderson	4811.
1 Chandbally, Orissa	C. H. Dreyer	12571.
4 Calcutta	J. Anderson	9873-5, 9934.
1 Botanical Gardens, Calcutta	J. Anderson	9977.
11 Alipore, Calcutta	V. Ball	9985-95.
1 Tupai Mukh	Luchai Exped.	2775.
1 Cherrapunji	Col. H. H. Godwin-Austen	10014.
5 Sibsagar	S. E. Peal	2779, 8968, 8970, 10029-30.
5 Samagooting, Naga hills	J. Butler	9996-7, 10009-11.
1 Hotha, Yunan	Yunan Exped. (Anderson)	4162.
1 Momien, Yunan	Yunan Exped. (Anderson)	4163.
2 2nd defile, Irrawady R.	Yunan Exped. (Anderson)	4261-2.
5 Mandalay	Major Sladen	9978-82.
6 Moulmein	F. Stoliczka	3556, 10004-8.
1 Amherst, Tenasserim	J. Armstrong	10013.
1 Mooleyit, Tenasserim	Tenasserim Exped. (Limborg)	4099.
1 Amiah, Tavoy	Tenasserim Exped. (Limborg)	12821.
6 Mergui	Mergui Exped. (Anderson)	11773-7, 11850.
2 Andamans	G. E. Dobson	8786-7.
3 Andamans	F. Stoliczka	3558-60.
2 Nicobars	F. Stoliczka	2787-8.
2 Penang	F. Stoliczka	3561, 9939.
2 Malacca	F. Stoliczka	3530, 10015.
2 Singapore	F. Stoliczka	2708, 3557.
1 Singapore	W. Davison	13340.
1 No loc.	No hist.	10932.

122. BUFO PARIETALIS, Boul.

Boulenger, Ind. Rept. p. 507 ; W. Sclater, P. Z. S. 1892, p. 347.
Distribution—Southern India and Southern China?

1 Hongkong	Dr. R. Hungerford	11950.

123. BUFO BIPORCATUS, Gravenh.

Boulenger, Ind. Rept. p. 507.
Distribution—Tenasserim and the Malay Peninsula, extending to Sumatra, Java, and Borneo.

2 Burma-Siam hills	Museum Collector	12790-1.
2 Tavoy, Mergui	Mergui Exped. (Anderson)	11772, 11778.
1 Mergui	Mergui Exped. (Anderson)	11817.
1 Malacca	W. Davison	13342.
1 Sinkip Isle, Sumatra	J. Wood-Mason	4229.

124. BUFO ASPER, Gravenh.

Boulenger, Ind. Rept. p. 507.
Distribution—Tenasserim, the Malay Peninsula, Sumatra, Java, and Borneo.

16 Taing, Mergui	Mergui Exped. (Anderson)	11753–68.
8 Lampee, Mergui	Mergui Exped. (Anderson)	11780–7.
1 Pilai, Mergui	Mergui Exped. (Anderson)	11779.
1 Jelebu, Malay Peninsula	Raffles Museum (Davison)	13341.

125. BUFO CALAMITA, Laur.

Boulenger, Cat. Batr. Sal. p. 293.
Distribution—Europe.

| 1 Galicia | G. A. Boulenger | 13070. |

126. BUFO REGULARIS, Reuss.

Boulenger, Cat. Batr. Sal. p. 298.
Distribution—Africa and Arabia.

4 Edfou, Upper Egypt	J. Anderson	11301–4.
2 Luxor, Egypt	J. Anderson	11272–3.
7 Egypt	J. Anderson	11274–80.

127. BUFO BLANFORDII, Boul.

Boulenger, Cat. Batr. Sal. p. 301.
Distribution—Abyssinia.

| 3 Lake Ashangi, Abyssinia, 8000 ft. | W. T. Blanford | 9865–7. |

128. BUFO SPINULOSUS, Wiegm.

Boulenger, Cat. Batr. Sal. p. 302.
Distribution—Chili and Peru.

| 1 Chili | E. Gerard [P.] | 12523. |

129. BUFO VULGARIS, Laur.

Boulenger, Cat. Batr. Sal. p. 303.
Distribution—The Palæarctic Region.

| Geneva | G. A. Boulenger | 13069. |
| 3 Lombardy | Prof. Cornalia [Ex.] | 9487–9. |

130. BUFO LENTIGINOSUS, Shaw.

Boulenger, Cat. Batr. Sal. p. 308.
Distribution—North America.

1 Lucknow, Ontario	Dr. J. H. Garnier [Ex.]	12291.
6 Ontario	Dr. J. H. Garnier [Ex.]	12179-80, 12187,
		12336, 12340-1.
1 Ontario (larva)	Dr. J. H. Garnier [Ex.]	12188.
1 No loc.	E. Gerard [P.]	12544.

131. BUFO VALLICEPS, Wiegm.

Boulenger, Cat. Batr. Sal. p. 319.
Distribution—Southern States and Central America.

1 Helotes, Texas	Dr. J. H. Garnier [Ex.]	12185.

132. COPHOPHRYNE SIKKIMENSIS (Bly.).

Boulenger, Ind. Rept. p. 508.
Distribution—Sikkim Himalayas.

2 Sikkim	Capt. W. S. Sherwill, A. S. B.	9854-5.
	(TYPES OF THE SPECIES, Bly.)	
1 Singalela Range, Sikkim, 12,000 ft.	W. S. Atkinson	2780.

Family HYLIDÆ.

133. CHOROPHILUS OCULARIS (Holb.).

Boulenger, Cat. Batr. Sal. p. 333.
Distribution—Southern States of N. America.

1 S. Diego, Texas	Dr. J. H. Garnier [Ex.]	12182.

134. CHOROPHILUS TRISERIATUS (Wied).

Boulenger, Cat. Batr. Sal. p. 335.
Distribution—Eastern parts of N. America.

3 Ontario	Dr. J. H. Garnier [Ex.]	12331-2, 12335.

135. ACRIS GRYLLUS (Leconte).

Boulenger, Cat. Batr. Sal. p. 336.
Distribution—N. America.

3 Ontario	Dr. J. H. Garnier [Ex.]	12334-4, 12337.
2 Mexico	Dr. J. H. Garnier [Ex.]	12148-9.

136. HYLA ANNECTENS (Jerdon).

Boulenger, Ind. Rept. p. 509.
Distribution—Hills of Assam and Yunan.

3 Khasia hills, Assam	T. C. Jerdon	10170-2.
	(TYPES OF THE SPECIES, Jerdon.)	
3 Khasia hills	Col. H. H. Godwin-Austen	10394-6.
9 Cherrapunji, Khasia hills	J. H. Bourne	9820, 10292-9.
1 Samagooting, Naga hills	J. Butler	10200.
36 Yunan	J. Anderson	10308-29, 10331-44.
2 No loc.	No hist., A. S. B.	10303-4.

137. HYLA BUCKLEYI, Boul.

Boulenger, Cat. Batr. Sal. p. 362.
Distribution—Ecuador.

1 Sarayacu, Ecuador	E. Gerard [P.]	12507.

138. HYLA VERSICOLOR, Leconte.

Boulenger, Cat. Batr. Sal. p. 372.
Distribution—Eastern North America.

4 Kent, Ontario	Dr. J. H. Garnier [Ex.]	12142-5.
3 Ontario	Dr. J. H. Garnier [Ex.]	12192, 12286-7.
1 N. Carolina	Rev. F. Fitzgerald, A. S. B.	2726.

139. HYLA CAROLINENSIS (Penn.).

Boulenger, Cat. Batr. Sal. p. 377.
Distribution—South-eastern States of North America.

1 No loc.	No hist.	10257.

140. HYLA ARBOREA (Linn.).

Boulenger, Cat. Batr. Sal. p. 379.
Distribution—The Palæarctic region, from France to Japan.

Subsp. typica.

2 Piedmont, Italy	Prof. Cornalia	10253-4.

Subsp. savignyi.

1 Damascus	J. Anderson	11325.
1 Baalbek, Cœlesyria	J. Anderson	11210.
2 Mt. Hermon, Palestine	J. Anderson	11194, 11206.
1 Plains of Jericho	J. Anderson	11343.
1 Basrah, Persia Gulf	W. T. Blanford	3520.
2 Resht, N. Persia	W. T. Blanford	3519, 3522.
1 Ghilan, Persia	W. T. Blanford	3521.
5 No loc.	No history	10315-9.

Subsp. **meridionalis.**

1 Bordeaux   G. A. Boulenger   13077.

Subsp. **japonica.**

1 Yezo, Japan   J. Anderson   13012.
3 Kiga, Japan   J. Anderson   13004-6

141. HYLA CHINENSIS, Günth.

Boulenger, Cat. Batr. Sal. p. 381.
Distribution—Southern China.

2 Amoy   Dr. Hungerford   11387 8.

142. HYLA PICKERINGII (Holbr.).

Boulenger, Cat. Batr. Sal. p. 399.
Distribution—Eastern North America.

1 Ontario   Dr. J. H. Garnier [Ex.]   12342.
3 Massachusetts   Dr. J. H. Garnier [Ex.]   12328-30.

143. HYLA LESUEURII, Dum. & Bibr.

Boulenger, Cat. Batr. Sal. p. 412.
Distribution—Australia.

1 Paramatta, N.S.W.   E. Gerard [P.]   12516.

144. NOTOTREMA MARSUPIATUM, Dum. & Bibr.

Boulenger, Cat. Batr. Sal. p. 416.
Distribution—Peru and Ecuador.

1 Ecuador   E. Gerard [P.]   12519.

Family PELOBATIDÆ.
145. SCAPHIOPUS COUCHII, Baird.

Boulenger, Cat. Batr. Sal. p. 434.
Distribution—Southern United States and Mexico.

1 Florida   Dr. J. H. Garnier [Ex.]   12181.

146. PELOBATES FUSCUS (Laur.).

Boulenger, Cat. Batr. Sal. p. 437.
Distribution—Central Europe.

2 Berlin   G. A. Boulenger   13055 6.
3 Mulanais   Prof. Cornalia [Ex.]   9479-81.

147. PELODYTES PUNCTATUS (Daud.).

Boulenger, Cat. Batr. Sal. p. 438.
Distribution—France, Spain, and Portugal.

2 Brittany	G. A. Boulenger	13053-4.

148. LEPTOBRACHIUM MONTICOLA (Günth.).

Boulenger, Ind. Rept. p. 510.
Distribution—Sikkim, Assam, and Burma.

6 Darjeeling	T. C. Jerdon	9673-7, 9721.
12 Darjeeling	J. Gammie	9650, 9668-72, 9681, 10776-80.
1 Khasia hills, Assam	T. C. Jerdon	9679.
75 Cherrapunji, Assam	J. H. Bourne	9692-709, 9711-15, 9717, 9726-38, 9740-76, 10823.
1 Burma	W. Theobald	10500.
1 No loc.	No hist., A. S. B.	10967.
	(Type of Ixalus lateralis. Anderson.)	
3 No loc.	No hist., A. S. B.	9125-6, 10046.

149. LEPTOBRACHIUM HASSELTII, Tschudi.

Boulenger, Ind. Rept. p. 511.
Distribution—Assam, Burma, the Malay Peninsula, Sumatra, Java,
and Borneo.

1 Cherrapunji	J. H. Bourne	10437.
2 Ahsoon, Tenass., 2000 ft.	Tenasserim Exped. (Limborg)	10439-40.
1 Lampee, Mergui	Mergui Exped. (Anderson)	11841.

150. LEPTOBRACHIUM CARINENSE, Boul.

Boulenger, Ind. Rept. p. 511 ; W. Sclater, P. Z. S. 1892, p. 347.
Distribution—Hills of Karenne and Tenasserim.

1 Mergui	Major Berdmore, A. S. B.	9840.

151. MEGALOPHRYS MONTANA (Kuhl).

Boulenger, Cat. Batr. Sal. p. 442.
Distribution—East-Indian Islands, Java, Borneo, and Sumatra.

1 Borneo	E. Gerard [P.]	12498.

D

Family DISCOGLOSSIDÆ.

152. DISCOGLOSSUS PICTUS, Otth.

Boulenger, Cat. Batr. Sal. p. 445.
Distribution—South Europe and North Africa.

3 Monte Cristo Isle, France   Prof. Giglioli [Ex.]   13363-5.

153. BOMBINATOR IGNEUS (Laur.).

Boulenger, Cat. Batr. Sal. p. 447.
Distribution—Palæarctic region.

3 Tyrol   Prof. Cornalia [Ex.]   9495-7.
3 Florence   Prof. Giglioli [Ex.]   13360-2.

154. ALYTES OBSTETRICANS (Laur.).

Boulenger, Cat. Batr. Sal. p. 448.
Distribution—France, Germany, and Switzerland.

6 Paris   G. A. Boulenger   13071-6.

Family DACTYLETHRIDÆ.

155. XENOPUS LÆVIS (Daud.).

Boulenger, Cat. Batr. Sal. p. 456.
Distribution—Tropical Africa.

1 Senafé, Tigré. Abyssinia   W. T. Blanford   9174.

Order II. CAUDATA.

Family SALAMANDRIDÆ.

156. SALAMANDRA MACULOSA (Linn.).

Boulenger, Cat. Batr. Caud. p. 3.
Distribution—Central and Southern Europe, N. Africa, and Asia Minor.

1 France   M. Malherbe, A. S. B.   10391.
3 Lake Como, Italy   Prof. Cornalia   10406-8.

157. MOLGE CRISTATA (Laur.).

Boulenger, Cat. Batr. Caud. p. 8.
Distribution—The greater part of Europe except Spain.

2 Milan	G. A. Boulenger	13041-2.
2 Lombardy	Prof. Cornalia	10403, 10405.

158. MOLGE MARMORATA (Latr.).

Boulenger, Cat. Batr. Caud. p. 11.
Distribution—France, Spain, and Portugal.

3 Bordeaux	G. A. Boulenger	13038-40.

159. MOLGE VULGARIS (Linn.).

Boulenger, Cat. Batr. Caud. p. 14.
Distribution—Europe, except France, Spain, and Portugal; temperate Asia.

3 London	G. A. Boulenger	13043-5.
7 England	H. Strickland, A. S. B.	10383-9.
2 Europe	Hungarian Mus. [Ex.]	10398-9.

160. MOLGE PALMATA (Schneid.).

Boulenger, Cat. Batr. Caud. p. 16.
Distribution—Western Europe from N. Spain to Germany.

4 Brussels	G. A. Boulenger	13046-9.
4 No loc.	No hist., A. S. B.	10418-21.

161. MOLGE PYRRHOGASTRA, Boie.

Boulenger, Cat. Batr. Caud. p. 19.
Distribution—Japan and China.

13 Hakone, Japan	J. Anderson	12969 81.
1 Lake Biwa, Japan	J. Anderson	12982.

162. MOLGE SINENSIS (Gray).

Boulenger, Cat. Batr. Caud. p. 20.
Distribution—Southern China.

1 Hongkong	Hongkong Mus. [Ex.]	12686.

163. MOLGE VIRIDESCENS (Rafin.).

Boulenger, Cat. Batr. Caud. p. 21.
Distribution—Eastern States of North America.

| 1 No loc. | No hist. | 10390. |

164. MOLGE MONTANA (Savi).

Boulenger, Cat. Batr. Caud. p. 23.
Distribution—Corsica.

| 5 Corsica | Prof. Giglioli [Ex.] | 13373-7. |

165. MOLGE RUSCONII, Gené.

Boulenger, Cat. Batr. Caud. p. 24.
Distribution—Sardinia.

| 2 Sardinia | Prof. Giglioli [Ex.] | 13378-9. |

166. SALAMANDRINA PERSPICILLATA (Savi).

Boulenger, Cat. Batr. Caud. p. 28.
Distribution—Switzerland and Italy.

2 Geneva	G. A. Boulenger.	13050-1.
2 Genoa	Prof. Cornalia [Ex.]	10392-3.
4 Florence	Prof. Giglioli [Ex.]	13369-72.

167. TYLOTOTRITON VERRUCOSUS, Anders.

Boulenger, Ind. Rept. p. 514.
Distribution—Hills of Sikkim, Upper Burma, and Yunan.

1 Sikkim	Col. Mainwaring	10397.
1 Mechi R., 6000 ft.,		
Darjeeling dist.	W. Helps	11396.
14 Momien, Yunan	Yunan Exped. (Anderson)	10366-79.
2 Ponsee, Kakhyen hills	Yunan Exped. (Anderson)	10380-1.

(16 TYPES OF THE SPECIES, Anders.).

168. HYNOBIUS NEBULOSUS, Schleg.

Boulenger, Cat. Batr. Caud. p. 32.
Distribution—Japan.

| 3 Yezo, Japan | J. Anderson | 12094-6. |

169. ONYCHODACTYLUS JAPONICUS, Houttuyn.

Boulenger, Cat. Batr. Caud. p. 35.
Distribution—Japan.

10 Hakone, Japan	J. Anderson	12983-92.

170. PLETHODON GLUTINOSUS (Green).

Boulenger, Cat. Batr. Caud. p. 56.
Distribution—Eastern States of N. America.

1 North Carolina	Rev. F. Fitzgerald. A. S. B.	10100.

171. SPELERPES RUBER (Daud.).

Boulenger, Cat. Batr. Caud. p. 63.
Distribution—Eastern States of N. America.

1 North Carolina	Rev. F. Fitzgerald, A. S. B.	2712.

172. SPELERPES FUSCUS (Bonap.).

Boulenger, Cat. Batr. Caud. p. 69.
Distribution—South France and Italy.

3 Florence	Prof. Giglioli [Ex.]	13366-8.

Family AMPHIUMIDÆ.

173. CRYPTOBRANCHUS ALLEGHANIENSIS (Daud.).

Boulenger, Cat. Batr. Caud. p. 81.
Distribution—Middle States of N. America.

1 Pennsylvania	Schneider [P.]	11472.
2 No loc.	Purchased	11377-8.

174. AMPHIUMA MEANS, Garden.

Boulenger, Cat. Batr. Caud. p. 83.
Distribution—South-eastern States of N. America.

2 S. Carolina	Rev. F. Fitzgerald, A. S. B.	10072-3.

Family PROTEIDÆ.

175. NECTURUS MACULATUS (Rafin.).

Boulenger, Cat. Batr. Caud. p. 84.
Distribution—Eastern parts of N. America.

1 Huron Co., Ontario	J. H. Garnier [Ex.]	12297.
1 Mississippi	Schneider [P.]	11474.
2 N. America	J. H. Garnier [Ex.]	12200, 12205.

176. PROTEUS ANGUINUS, Laur.

Boulenger, Cat. Batr. Caud. p. 85.
Distribution—Subterranean waters of the Alps of Carniola.

| 1 Adelsberg, Carniola | Prof. Cornalia [Ex.] | 10411. |
| 1 No loc. | No hist. | 10423. |

Family SIRENIDÆ.

177. SIREN LACERTINA, Linn.

Boulenger, Cat. Batr. Caud. p. 87.
Distribution—South-east States of N. America.

| 1 S. Carolina | Schneider [P.] | 11474. |
| 1 Louisiana | J. H. Garnier [Ex.] | 12705. |

Order III. APODA.

Family CŒCILIIDÆ.

178. ICHTHYOPHIS GLUTINOSUS (Linn.).

Boulenger, Ind. Rept. p. 515.
Distribution—Hills of Southern India and Ceylon, Sikkim, Assam, Burma, Siam, Malay Peninsula and Archipelago.

5 Koppa, Mysore	W. M. Daly	13546-9, 13566.
1 Anamalai hills (larva)	Col. R. H. Beddome	4448.
1 Anamalai hills	Col. R. H. Beddome	8761.
1 Travancore	Col. R. H. Beddome	4376.
3 S. India	Col. R. H. Beddome	10422, 10414-5.
1 Ceylon	Col. R. H. Beddome	4413.
1 Ceylon	H. Nevill	6977.
1 Ceylon	W. Ferguson	10417.

2 Darjeeling	J. Gammie	10109-10.
2 Goalpara, Assam	H. L. Haughton, A. S. B.	10402 3.
1 Cherrapunji	J. H. Bourne	10416.
1 Tavoy	C. E. Pitman	12870.
1 Siam	Hongkong Mus. [Ex.]	12684.

179. ICHTHYOPHIS MONOCHROUS, Bleek.

Boulenger. Ind. Rept. p. 517.
Distribution—Western Ghats, Sikkim, Tenasserim, Malay Peninsula and Islands.

| 1 Tenasserim | Major Berdmore. A. S. B. | 10401. |

180. URÆOTYPHLUS OXYURUS (Dum. & Bibr.).

Boulenger, Ind. Rept. p. 517.
Distribution—South India.

| 2 No loc. | Col. R. H. Beddome [Ex.] | 4391, 10412. |

INDEX.

Printed by TAYLOR and FRANCIS, Red Lion Court, Fleet Street.